Ole & Lena

A Stud and a Hot Dish

Featuring

Bruce Danielson as Ole and Ann Berg as Lena

Adventure Publications, Inc.
Cambridge, MN

PHOTO CREDITS

Cover photos by Ryan Jacobson

All photos are copyright Ryan Jacobson unless otherwise noted.
Shutterstock: 18, 34, 46, 93 **Sam Toward:** 94 (Bruce's Biography)
Carlson Studio of Photography: 94 (Ann's Biography)

Edited by Ryan Jacobson

Cover and book design by Jonathan Norberg

10 9 8 7 6 5 4 3

Copyright 2007 by Bruce Danielson and Ann Berg
Published by Adventure Publications, Inc.
820 Cleveland St. S
Cambridge, MN 55008
1-800-678-7006
www.adventurepublications.net

817.54
OLE   *OCLC*   *5/25/11*

Printed in the U.S.A.

ISBN-13: 978-1-59193-203-1
ISBN-10: 1-59193-203-3

DEDICATIONS

Bruce Danielson: I dedicate this book to the thousands of people who have attended the faculty variety show over the past nineteen years and to everyone who has attended our performances around the country. It is because of that show and because of *YOU* that Ann and I have performed as Ole and Lena for all of this time. I sincerely love playing the character of Ole. His crazy antics and his innocent outlook on life have brought me an enormous amount of joy and laughter. It will be a sad day for me when I hang up the flannel shirt and plaid hat and say, "Goodbye," to this good friend. Thanks to all!

Ann Berg: This book is dedicated to my students. Thank you for filling every day with laughter and the love of learning. You're the best!

Ole and Lena: Ve dedicate dis book to Bruce Danielson and Ann Berg. If dey *REALLY* tink anyvon is goin' to buy dis book, dey are even dummer dan ve tink dey are.

ACKNOWLEDGEMENTS

Thanks to the following students, friends and colleagues who appeared in the book: Page 14: Dr. Lowell Becker; Page 20: Jett Serie; Page 22: Tim Kosel; Page 22, 30, 76 and 80: Elizabeth Nault-Maurer; Page 24: Justin Nelson; Page 24, 26, 30 and 36: Benjamin Nault-Maurer; Page 32 and 42: Cal Blakesly; Page 36: Craig Prihoda, Matt Jakubiec, Burke Lindvall; Page 44: Bob Hansen; Page 50: Frank Wells, Jack Hammargren; Page 54 and 58: Wade Book; Page 56: Steve Miller; Page 64: Dave Maurer; Page 70: Kris Christiansen; Page 72: District Judge James E. Dehn; Page 74: Linda Pearson, Bill Kruschel, Becky Lieser; Page 82: Joyce Swanson, Lois Salo, Mary Falk, Delores Oslund, Norma Carlson, Darlene Fixell.

Thanks to the following businesses and friends who lent supplies or locations and made this book possible: Cambridge-Isanti High School, Cambridge Launderers & Cleaners, Cambridge Lutheran Church, Cambridge Medical Center, Cambridge Middle School, Bob Hansen, Isanti County Government Center, Isanti County Sheriff's Department, Lumberland Home Center, Parker Satrom & Donegan PA, Perkins Restaurant & Bakery, Purple Hawk Country Club, Steve's Tire, Wolcyn Tree Farms.

A special thank you to Ryan Jacobson for his creative, photographic and technical skills that added so much to the aesthetic quality of the photographs and the imaginative quality of the book. Your input was invaluable.

FOREWORD

Ole and Lena tried to get someone famous to write their foreword—you know, like other famous books do. They contacted Bill Cosby, whom they worked with in Minot, North Dakota, at Hostfest. He replied, "Ole and Lena who?" They tried to get Charley Pride, whom they shared a stage with for four days straight. He wrote back, "Kiss an angel good morning, but avoid Lena like the plague!" They finally contacted the Norwegian Embassy in Washington, D.C., which declared, "We'll write anything they want if they'll only admit they're Swedish!" So, as usual, Ole and Lena will write their own foreword, but they insist on writing it backward.

The real-life Ole and Lena (Bruce Danielson and Ann Berg) have worked together for nearly twenty years, telling and retelling the stories of their two favorite Scandinavians. After writing their first book, Ole and Lena: Live Via Satellite, they traveled twice to Minot, North Dakota, for Hostfest, all the way to Montana to be Grand Marshals of the Norticfest parade, and to various places throughout Minnesota, Wisconsin and Iowa. However, their first love remains performing at their annual faculty variety show, where the teacher's union has raised nearly $150,000 to be awarded as scholarships to aspiring teachers. Bruce and Ann love to perform, and they love to hear the sound of laughter. So if you enjoy this book, laugh REALLY loud so they can hear you all the way to Cambridge, Minnesota.

TABLE OF CONTENTS

Life vit da Olsons

(In what library section do you file this book?
Adventure? Humor? Constipation?)

Ole: I tink you're goin' to need a second coat.

LENA'S AGE

Ole: I understand you're not admittin' to your real age. Few vemen admit dere age.

Lena: Yah, vell, few men act deres!

Ole: Lena says her age is nobody's business. Let's yust say she's been *IN* business a long time.

Lena: I'm approachin' forty.

Ole: Yah, from vich direction?

Ole: Lena put on a mudpack last veek. She looked good for four days. Den da mudpack fell off.

Lena: Ole, do you tink I'll lose my looks ven I get older?

Ole: Vell, if you're lucky, yes.

Lena: I'm exercisin' to get in shape.

Ole: You're already in shape. Dat shape is round!

LENA'S WEIGHT

Lena: I've kept my figure all dese years.

Ole: Yah, no von else vanted it.

Ole: I von't say Lena is heavy, but ven she vears red earrings, she looks like da back end of a bus.

Ole: How much does Lena weigh? One hundred and *PLENTY*!

Ole: I don't mind Lena's weight. She's da only investment I ever made dat doubled in size.

Lena's doctor told her that she should stop watching golf on television and get more exercise. So now she watches tennis.

Ole: Lena spent four hours in da beauty shop da udder day, and dat vas yust for da estimate!

Ole: Lena, vould you look in my ear? I can't hear you.

Lena: Ole, you've got a suppository stuck in dere.

Ole: Vell, dat explains vere my hearin' aid vent.

Lena: At least now you can hear yourself tink.

OLE'S BAD HABITS

Lena: No von makes a fool of Ole. He's da do-it-yourself type.

Whenever Ole came home a little "tipsy," he was always a heavy snorer. That bothered Lena. So one night, when Ole crawled into bed after a late evening with the boys, she tied a big, blue ribbon around his nose. It worked. Ole stopped snoring immediately.

The next morning Lena asked, "Vere did you go last night?"

"I don't remember," said Ole, looking in the mirror, "but wherever it vas, I von first prize."

Ole bought a birthday cake for his brother and wanted to write "happy birthday" on it. Unfortunately, he couldn't figure out how to get the cake into the typewriter.

Lena: Ole has a bad habit of bitin' his nails.

Tina: Lots of people do dat, Lena.

Lena: Dere his *TOE* nails!

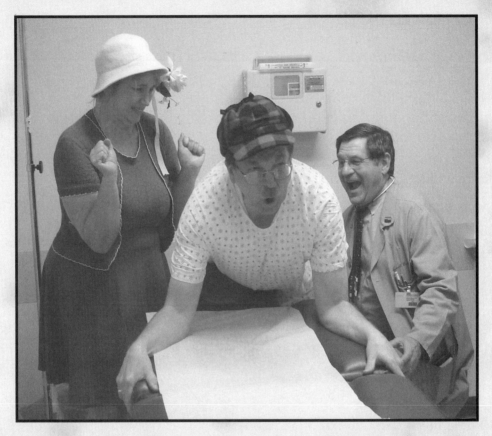

Lena: Ole's been really constipated since he started dat construction job.

Doctor: Ole, empty cement bags are not a good substitute for toilet paper.

OLE'S HEALTH CONCERNS

Ole went to see the doctor, but the doctor could find nothing wrong with him.

"It must be from the effects of drinking," the doctor stated.

"Vell, den," said Ole, "I'll come back ven you're sober."

Ole and Lena's sex life wasn't going well, so Ole visited a doctor. The doctor told Ole that he needed some exercise. He suggested that Ole walk ten miles a day and call in one week.

A week later the phone rang, and sure enough, it was Ole.

"How's the sex life?" the doctor asked.

"Not so good," Ole said. "I'm seventy miles away from home."

Ole: Doctor, da pills you gave me for B.O. are not verkin'.

Doctor: What's wrong with them?

Ole: Dey keep slippin' out from under my arms.

Ole: I fell down da stairs, and now it hurts ven I touch my head, my legs, my stomach and my chest.

Doctor: Of course it does. You've broken your finger.

Lena: Ole, tell me da truth. Who vas your first love?

Ole: It vas my second grade teacher, but it didn't verk out. I vas twelve years older dan her.

OLE & LENA—YOUNG LOVE

Lena: Ven ve ver datin', Ole and I almost froze to death at da drive-in movie. Ve ver vatchin' *Closed for da Season*.

Young Lena: Ole, do you love me vit all your heart and soul?

Young Ole: Uh-huh.

Young Lena: Do you tink I'm da most beautiful girl in da verld?

Young Ole: Uh-huh.

Young Lena: Do you tink my lips are like rose petals?

Young Ole: Uh-huh.

Young Lena: Ole, you say da most romantic tings!

Ole: Da janitor in dis apartment building is such a braggart. He claims to haf kissed every voman in da whole building except von.

Lena: It must be dat snooty Mrs. Peterson on da first floor.

Soon after Ole and Lena were married, Ole noticed that their credit card had been stolen. He decided not to report it though. The thief charged less than Lena did.

YOU KNOW LENA IS COOKING WHEN...

- Ole refers to the smoke detector as the oven timer.

- Ole and Lena's after-dinner drink is Pepto-Bismol.

- Little Ole goes outside to make mud pies; the rest of the family grabs forks and follows him.

- The kids come in for dinner every time they hear a fire siren.

- The army's interested in Lena's homemade biscuits—to use as mortar fire.

- Trust us, you don't *WANT* to know when Lena is cooking!

WARNING

If you see this woman anywhere near a kitchen, contact us immediately.

The Fire Department

School Days vit da Olsons

(Fifth grade—the best four years of Ole's life)

Lena: Littlest Ole is makin' straight A's.

Ole: Yah, but his B's are crooked.

LITTLEST OLE'S SCHOOL WOES

Teacher: Let's see if you can get this one, Littlest Ole. What is the capital of Wisconsin?

Littlest Ole: W?

Ole: I hope you can go to college some day, Littlest Ole. I vanted to go, but yust one little ting kept me from it.

Littlest Ole: Vat vas dat, Papa?

Ole: High school.

Littlest Ole: Mama, remember dat $20 you'd give me for passin' math?

Lena: Yah.

Littlest Ole: I yust saved you $20.

Littlest Ole: Papa, at da baseball playoffs today, I vas responsible for da winnin' run!

Ole: Dat's wonderful! Vat did you do?

Littlest Ole: I dropped da ball.

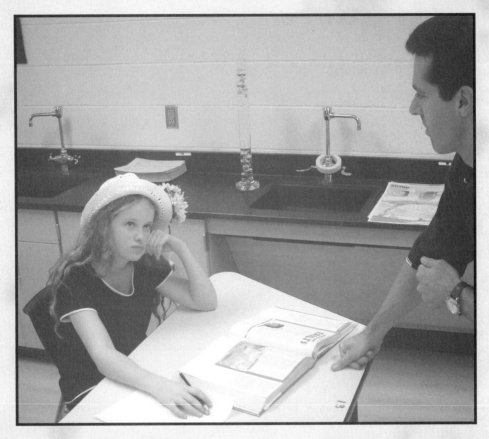

Teacher: Now, Little Lena, if you're in a vacuum and someone calls your name, will you hear it?

Little Lena: Is da vacuum on or off?

LITTLE LENA'S CONFUSION

Little Lena once tried to alphabetize a bag of M&Ms.

Little Lena called a friend and arranged to meet her at the corner of "walk" and "don't walk."

When Little Lena started wearing makeup, she put lipstick on her forehead. She wanted to make up her mind.

Little Lena came running into the house waving her latest math paper.

"Mom, I did great on dis paper," she said. "Dere ver only three mistakes on it. You made one, Papa made one, and I made one."

Little Lena: Teacher, vy do ve see dogs vearin' sveaters but never goldfish vearin' bathin' trunks?

Little Lena: Teacher, if da Number Two pencil is da most popular, vy is it still Number Two?

Teacher: Suppose I asked you to meet me for lunch at 23 degrees 4 minutes north latitude and 45 degrees 15 minutes east longitude?

Little Ole: Vell, I guess you'd be eatin' alone.

LITTLE OLE'S SCHOOL TROUBLES

Lena: It's such a nice day. I tink I'll take Little Ole to da zoo.

Ole: I vouldn't bodder. If dey vant him, dey can come and get him.

Little Ole called his mama from a friend's house and told her that he had broken a lamp.

"Ve von't have to buy dem a new von, doh," he added. "Dey said it vas irreplaceable."

Teacher: Little Ole, your answer is not right. "H, I, J, K, L, M, N, O" is *NOT* the formula for water.

Little Ole: Vell, you said vater vas H to O.

Little Ole brought home a report card with four F's and one D.

"Vell," said Ole, "it looks like you're spendin' too much time on von subject."

Teacher: Where is the English Channel?

Little Ole: I dunno. Ve don't haf cable.

Lena: You can't fool me Little Ole. You skipped school yesterday and played baseball.

Little Ole: Mama, I never skipped school to play baseball, and I have da fish to prove it.

LITTLE OLE'S SCHOOL TROUBLES 2

Teacher: Little Ole, you missed school yesterday, didn't you?

Little Ole: Not very much.

Little Ole: My teacher vas mad at me because I didn't know vere da Rockies ver.

Lena: Vell, next time remember vere you put tings!

Little Ole: Papa, can you help me? I haf to find da lowest common denominator.

Ole: You mean to tell me dey haven't found dat yet? Dey vas lookin' for dat ven I vas a boy.

Little Ole was late for Sunday morning confirmation class. He told his teacher that he was going to go fishing, but his papa decided at the last minute that it was more important to go to church.

"That's very impressive, Little Ole," said the teacher. "Did your father tell you why going to church is more important than fishing?"

"Yah," answered Little Ole, "Papa said he didn't have enough bait for da both of us."

Please execute
Little Ole from
skool yesterrdae.
He had very
loose vowels and
a sore trout.
Cinseerly,
Little Ole's Dad

Outdoor Life

(Duck hunting troubles? Maybe you
aren't throwing the dog high enough.)

Little Lena: How come you're catchin' all da fish, Little Ole?

Little Ole: Hmm whjmm inmm.

Little Lena: I can't hear you so good.

Little Ole: Ymmm gmmm tmm.

Little Lena: Vat did you say?

Little Ole: I said, ya gotta keep your vorms varm.

OLE AND FISHING

Lena: How vas fishin'?

Ole: Da fishin' vas good, Lena. Da catchin' vas lousy, doh.

Lena: Ven Ole goes fishin', it's a jerk at von end of da line vaitin' for a jerk at da udder!

Ole and Sven rented a boat from a nearby resort and had great luck fishing.

On the way home, Ole said to Sven, "How are ve goin' to find dat same fishin' spot again?"

"Vell," said Sven, "I marked da boat vit an X, so ve can find da right place."

"Uffda, dat vas dumb," Ole said. "Vat if ve don't get dat same boat again?"

Lena: Remember Ole: Ven you come back from fishin', I'm vaitin' to hear doze three little vords I like to hear.

Ole: Oh, yah, "Is dinner ready?"

Sven and Ole didn't win the ice fishing contest, but they're certain the other guys cheated. They cut holes in the ice.

OLE AND FISHING 2

Sven and Ole were ice fishing with Lena. On the way home, Lena and Ole sat in the front and Sven was in the back when the truck crashed through the ice. Ole and Lena popped out of the water, and Sven finally appeared too.

Ole asked him, "Vat took you so long?"

"Vell," said Sven, "I had trouble gettin' da tailgate open."

Lena and Ole went fishing together one time, and this is what happened:

Lena: Do you haf anodder cork dat I can use as a bobber, Ole? Dis von keeps sinkin'.

Ole and Sven rented a boat, and they bought some bait, lures, lunch and gas. After a long day of poor fishing, they headed back to the dock.

Ole tallied up their expenses and declared, "Dese two fish cost us $80 apiece!"

"Uffda," said Sven, "at dat price it's a good ting ve didn't catch more."

Sven: Ole, since Noah vas surrounded by vater, do you imagine he fished a lot?

Ole: How could he? He only had two vorms.

Ole called the DNR to have the deer crossing signs near
his house moved. Too many deer were being hit by cars,
and he thought they should cross somewhere else.

OLE AND HUNTING

Ole was out hunting when he stumbled into his friend Torvald. "I am SO glad to see you, Torvald! I've been wanderin' around lost for two hours. I vas startin' to get scared."

"Dat's nottin'," said Torvald. "I've been lost for two days."

Ole and Sven went moose hunting in Canada. A pilot dropped them off then picked them up two days later. The duo had bagged a moose, but the pilot told them not to pack the antlers because they were too heavy.

Ole said, "Last year's pilot let us take dem."

So the pilot changed his mind, and they flew off with the antlers in tow.

Almost immediately, they crashed back to the ground. After the dust settled, Ole, the pilot and Sven assessed the wreckage.

"Vell," said Sven, "ve made it about a hundred yards furder dan last year."

Ole and Sven went goose hunting. After being out all day, it was starting to get dark, and Sven and Ole couldn't find their car.

Ole said, "I tink ve're lost."

"How do you know?" asked Sven.

"Vell," said Ole, "I've been lost before, and dis is vat it looks like."

Sven: My son's da star quarterback.

Torvald: My son's da team's best runnin' back.

Ole: Vell, da coach told me dat Little Ole is dere number von "drawback."

Winter (Uffda!)

(Ole got a great deal on snow tires.
It's too bad they melted on his way home.)

Ole: Dat's it, Lena. Ve're cuttin' down da next
Christmas tree vedder it's got lights on it or not!

OLE & LENA AND CHRISTMAS

Ole bought Lena a cell phone for Christmas. It rang when she was shopping for groceries.

"Do you like your phone?" asked Ole.

"Yah," said Lena, "but how did you know I vas at da grocery store?"

Lena: Ole tinks dat vit all da cold air comin' in from Canada in da vinter, dey should yust weatherstrip da border.

Ole: Lena didn't haf much luck Christmas shoppin' today. Dere vas a power failure at da mall, and she vas stuck on da escalator for hours.

Lars: Vy didn't she yust valk down?

Ole: She vas goin' up.

On the day after Christmas, Sven and Ole decided to try ice fishing. They bought bait, tackle and fishing gear at a little bait shop. They also got an ice pick. Two hours later they stopped back and asked for a dozen more ice picks.

"How are you fellows doing?" the shopkeeper asked.

"Not so good," said Sven. "Ve haven't even got da boat in da vater yet."

Ole: Lena, did you hear da von about da voman vit von leg? She vorked at IHOP.

Lena: Ole, did you hear da von about da lazy Norvegian? He got a shovel full of snow right in da...

OLE & LENA AND BAD WEATHER

Ole worried about Lena driving home during a blizzard, so he told her to always follow a snowplow. That would help to ensure her safety.

When the big snowstorm came, that's just what Lena did. She followed the snowplow's taillights for more than two hours, until it finally stopped moving.

The driver jumped out of the snowplow and ran back to Lena's car. "I've finished with the mall's parking lot," he told her. "Do you want to follow me to the grocery store?"

Ole came into the kitchen crying. "It's terrible, Lena. My papa vas yust struck by da snowplow vile he vas out shovelin' in da blizzard."

The phone rang again, and Ole came back crying even harder. "Dat vas my brodder Lars. His papa vas yust hit by da same darn snowplow!"

After a big snowstorm, the radio announced that it was a snow emergency so everyone should park on the east side of the street. Ole moved his car.

The next day, the radio announced that the snow emergency was continuing and that everyone should move their cars to the west side of the street. Again, Ole complied.

On the third day, no announcements were made. Ole decided, "Since dey von't tell us vich side of da street to park on, I'll yust leave da car in da garage."

Sven saw Ole shoveling his car out of the ditch.
He called, "Ole, vy don't I buy us some
coffee, and den I'll help you wit your truck."

"I don't tink Lena vould like dat," said Ole.

"Is she vaitin' at home?" asked Sven.

"No," Ole answered, "she's under da truck."

OLE & LENA'S KNOCK-KNOCK JOKES

Ole loves knock-knock jokes—especially winter ones.

Knock! Knock!
Who's there?

Snow.
Snow who?
Snow skating today; the ice is too thin.

Mandy.
Mandy who?
Mandy lifeboats; the ship has hit an iceberg!

Freeze.
Freeze who?
Freeze a jolly good fellow! Freeze a jolly good fellow!

Guitar.
Guitar who?
Guitar coats; it's cold outside.

Igloo.
Igloo who?
Igloo knew Suzie like I know Suzie...

Howard.
Howard who?
Howard you like to stand out in the cold while some idiot
keeps asking, "Who's there?"

Man: That's a strange hood ornament you have there.

Lena: It's a snow blower.

Man: A what?

Lena: Park da truck, Ole. Ve've finally driven far enough south.

OLE & LENA'S WINTER VACATIONS

Ole and Lena went on a second honeymoon. As they checked in, the manager asked if Ole wanted Dom Perignon sent to the room.

"No," Ole said, "I tink it vill yust be da two of us."

Sven: Vere are you two goin' on your vacation?

Ole: Yellowstone National Park.

Sven: Don't forget Old Faithful.

Ole: She's comin' vit me.

Ole: I vent on a real pleasure trip dis veekend.

Sven: Vere did you go?

Ole: I took my modder-in-law to da airport.

On his last plane trip, Ole was told to use gum to keep his ears from popping. But Ole didn't like it. He was picking gum out of his ears for a week.

Question: Vy dus it take so long to build a
Norvegian snowman?

Answer: You haf to hollow out da head.

Ole, Still Unemployed

(Ole's looking for a job with shorter hours,
but it seems all of them have sixty minutes.)

Ole was fired from working at the golf course.
He kept filling all of the holes.

OLE AND THE JOBS HE'S LOST

Ole: I don't know vy I am alvays gettin' fired. I'm a steady verker.

Sven: Yah, Ole, if you ver any steadier you'd be motionless.

When Ole takes a coffee break, it can't be longer than fifteen minutes. Otherwise, he needs to be completely retrained.

Ole wanted to be a mailman, but first he had to take an aptitude test.

An hour or so into it, Ole came across the question: "How far is it to the moon?"

Ole jumped out of his seat and stormed outside, grumbling, "If dat's vere I'm deliverin' da mail, dan I don't even vant dis job!"

Ole: I lost my job because of illness and fatigue. My boss got sick and tired of me.

Ole lost his job as an elevator operator when he couldn't learn the route.

Ole failed the construction exam.
When it asked, "What is stucco?" he wrote,
"Stucco is vat you get ven you sit on gummo."

OLE'S JOB SKILLS

Lena: Nobody can call Ole a quitter. He alvays gets fired.

Ole: Dere are three kinds of people in dis verld: dose who can count and dose who can't.

Lena: Ole has been called a "miracle verker" because ven he verks it's a miracle.

Ole: Help me stand, Lena. My verk injury is actin' up again.

Lena: Da only verk injury you got is a blister on your remote control thumb.

Lena: Dey gave Ole two orders on his last job: Get out and stay out.

Boss: We want a responsible person for this job.

Ole: Den I'm your man. All da udder jobs I verked at, venever anyting vent wrong, dey told me I vas responsible.

Ole finally got an office job. Here he is,
heading to work with his new Norwegian briefcase.

Drivin' vit da Olsons

(Lena's had so many moving violations
that they gave her a *SEASON* ticket!)

A police officer was astonished to see Lena driving along, KNITTING! He drove alongside her, calling "Pull over!"

"No," Lena called back, "sveater!"

LENA'S BAD DRIVING

Lena locked her keys in the car. It took her two hours to get the door unlocked and let Ole out.

Lena: Ole, I've been so nervous about my upcomin' driver's test dat I dreamed I vas a muffler last night. I voke up exhausted!

Lena: I can't get da car started. I tink it's flooded.

Ole: I'll check it. Vere is it?

Lena: In Peterson Lake.

Ole: Yup, it's flooded.

Officer: Ma'am, could I see your driver's license?

Lena: I vish you guys vould get your act togeder. Yesterday, anodder officer took avay my license, and den today you vant me to show it to you.

Ole and Lena's pickup truck is in rough shape. Instead of an air bag, there's a whoopee cushion duct-taped to the steering wheel.

Mechanic: It's running fine, now.

Ole: Vat vas da problem?

Mechanic: Just crap in the carburetor.

Ole: How often do I haf to do dat?

OLE'S DRIVING WOES

Ole and Sven were driving in a camper that was thirteen feet high when they stopped at an underpass. They saw a sign that read, "Low bridge. No vehicles over twelve feet."

"Vat do you tink, Sven?" asked Ole.

"Vell, dere's no cops around," Sven answered. "I say ve hit da gas pedal and go for it."

Ole attended a fancy party and was surprised to learn that neckties were required. Ole didn't even own a tie, so he wrapped his jumper cables around his neck and attempted to enter the party.

The host hesitated when he saw the cables but finally said, "Okay, Ole, you can come inside. But don't START anything."

Little Ole: Before you married Mama, who told you how to drive?

Sven and Ole were pumping gas, when Sven said, "Boy, dese gas prices sure are gettin' to me. I'll bet dere goin' to go even higher."

Ole replied, "It won't bodder me. I yust put $20 in dere, anyvay."

The police officer pulled Lena over after
seeing her car weaving from side to side.

Lena reported, "I vas swervin' to avoid da trees."

"Mrs. Olson," said the officer, "that's your air freshener."

LENA'S BAD DRIVING 2

Lena: Ole, I got a little, tiny scratch on da bumper.

Ole: Let's see da bumper, Lena.

Lena: Okay, it's in da trunk.

Lena was heading down the highway when her new cell phone rang. It was Ole.

"Better be careful, Lena," advised Ole. "Dere's somevon on your highvay drivin' da wrong vay."

"Somevon," Lena said, "dere's hundreds of 'em!"

Lena went to get gas and forgot the gas cap on top of the car. By the time she got home, it had fallen off. Ole told Lena he'd drive her car back to the gas station to see if he could find another one. He came back shortly.

"Ve lucked out, Lena. Dere vas anodder gas cap somevon else had left, and dis von is even better. It has a lock on it."

Ole and Lena's truck is in such rough shape that, whenever they stop at a light, people rush over to see if anyone is hurt.

OLE & LENA'S NEW ARRIVAL

Nurse: Mr. Olson, may I ask why you and Lena drove to the hospital in separate cars?

Ole: Dat vas my idea. I figured if ve got stuck in traffic, at least von of us vould get here in time. By da vay, is dere any news yet?

Nurse: Yes, Mr. Olson, Lena's had her baby. Would you like to guess what she had?

Ole: Vell, I hope it's a girl.

Nurse: No, it's a boy.

Ole: Dat's okay. Dat vas my second choice. Lena bet me $100 dat da baby vill look like her side of da family, and I bet $100 it vould look like my side. So vich side does he look like?

Nurse: To be honest, Mr. Olson, all newborns look like baby monkeys.

Ole: Oh, good, dan I vin. But I vonder, does da new baby look at *ALL* like me?

Nurse: Well, when you hold him a certain way he does indeed look like you. But we can't hold him that way long, or the blood rushes to his head.

Ole: Do I get to see da new baby some time soon?

Nurse: Your wife asked that we wait until the baby is a little older, a little stronger and can stand the shock.

Ole: Dat Lena, she tinks of everyting.

Relations of da Olson Family

(It takes an Olson family reunion to
get a total IQ score of a hundred.)

Ole: *ISH!* Here's da picture of Ingeborg at da Miss Nort Dakota Beauty Pageant.

Lena: Yah, Ole, she nearly von.

Ole: Nearly? She missed by at least two feet: twelve inches on dis hip and twelve inches on dat hip.

LENA'S SISTER INGEBORG

Lena: My sister Ingeborg is very kind to animals.

Ole: Yah? Den she should give her face back to da gorilla.

Lena: Ven ve ver younger, Ingeborg's best feature vas alvays her chin.

Ole: Now it's a *DOUBLE* feature.

Lena: I often tell Ingeborg dat she looks like a million bucks.

Ole: Da problem is dat it's all in loose change.

Lena: Vy can't you arrange a date for Ingeborg?

Ole: None of my friends vill date outside dere species.

Ole: Ingeborg has so many chins; she should be careful not to burp. It vould start a tsunami!

Ole: Ingeborg refused to marry a man von time, and he drank for a year and a haf. Now, I call dat carryin' a celebration too far.

Ole's brother Lars has a terrible memory.
It's so bad that when he uses the bathroom he has
to whistle—so he remembers which end to wipe.

OLE'S BROTHER LARS

Lena: Ole, in da Olson family tree, your brodder is da sap.

Lena: Lars is so dense dat it takes him an hour and a half to watch *60 Minutes*.

Lars is so dumb. He read in the newspaper that most accidents happen within twenty-five miles of home, so he moved.

Lars is so dumb. He read that smoking was bad for his health, so he gave up reading.

Lars won a big lottery jackpot. He was asked to attend a press conference to announce his good fortune.

"Will this change your life?" asked a local reporter.

"Nah, I'll yust do da same tings I've alvays done," answered Lars.

The reporter asked, "What about all of the letters begging for money?"

"Vell," said Lars, "I'll send dem out yust like usual."

Ole: Lena, here comes your sister. She's livin' proof of reincarnation. No von could get dat ugly in von lifetime.

LENA'S SISTER INGEBORG 2

Lena: Ingeborg is a very good housekeeper.

Ole: Yah, in all three divorces, she's kept da house.

Ole: Let's face it, Lena. Your sister eats so much dey use her picture on food stamps.

Ole: Ven Ingeborg steps on a scale, it says, "Von at a time, please."

Ole: Ingeborg is so ugly dat she vent into a haunted house and came out vit an application.

Ole: I never forget a face, but in Ingeborg's case I'll make an exception.

Ole: Ingeborg can't fit into a dress. She can't even fit into a dressin' room!

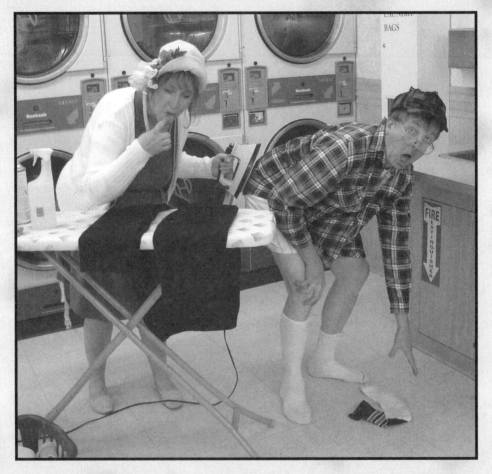

Ole hoped Lena could get out all
of the wrinkles—except that one.

At Home vit da Olsons

(How Swede it is—I mean Norwegian.)

Ole: I need some two-by-fours.

Worker: How long you need 'em?

Ole: A long time, ve're buildin' a garage.

OLE AROUND THE HOUSE

Lena got Ole an electric lawn mower for Father's Day. Now Ole can use the cord to find his way back to the house.

Ole: Venever Lena and I fight, she alvays gets historical.

Sven: You mean hysterical?

Ole: No, historical. She's alvays diggin' up my past.

Lars came to visit Ole and found him in the back yard digging his third hole for a new outhouse.

"Ole, I tought you ver yust goin' to haf a one-hole outhouse."

"I am," said Ole, "but da first two holes veren't deep enough."

Lena: Ole, I baked two kinds of cookies. Take your pick.

Ole: Thanks Lena, but I'll yust use my hammer.

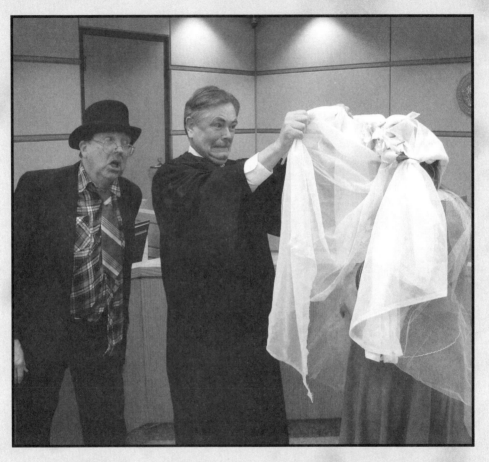

Ole: Lena and I ver married by a judge.
I should have asked for a jury.

OLE & LENA AND MARRIAGE

Marriage is a partnership. Ole is the silent partner.

Sven: My vife alvays has da last vord.

Ole: You're lucky. Mine never gets to it.

Ole: Lena told me she vanted a hot night and to be held close, so I brought her an electric blanket and a girdle.

Lena: My niece, Little Anna, really vants a husband.

Tina: She's obviously never had von.

Lena: Ole, you look tired. How 'bout a nice, big steak, mashed potatoes and apple pie for dessert?

Ole: No tanks, Lena. I'm too tired. Let's yust eat at home.

Ole never believed in hell. But ever since the wedding, Lena and her mother have shown him just how wrong he was.

Ole: I'd like two eggs runny, burnt toast and weak coffee.

Waitress: I don't understand, sir. That sounds terrible.

Ole: Lena's out of town, and I kinda miss her cookin'.

LENA'S BAD COOKING

Ole: You know vat dey say, "Ven dere's smoke, dere's Lena cookin'."

Ole: Lena has four special vays of servin' food: takeout, leftover, frozen and canned.

Ole: Lena doesn't like to cook at home. No von's invented a steak dat vill fit in da toaster.

Ole: Lena can't even make Jell-O. She can't figure out how to get two cups of vater into dat tiny packet.

Ole walked into the kitchen one day to find Lena crying.

Lena: Ole, dat cake I baked for you, da dog ate it!

Ole: Dat's okay, Lena. I'll get you anodder dog.

Ole: Lena's been cookin' a turkey for two and a half days. It said a half hour per pound, and Lena weighs 180.

SQUARE lefse? Only Lena...

OLE & LENA'S FAMILY AND FRIENDS

Ole: Da only part of Lena's modder dat ever gets sunburned is her tongue.

Ole: Lena, if I didn't love you so much, I vouldn't haf put up vit havin' your Aunt Enga stay vit us all summer.

Lena: My Aunt Enga? I tought she vas your Aunt Enga.

Ole and Sven went to their friend's funeral. They were looking at him in the casket when Sven said, "He sure looks good, doesn't he?"

"He should," said Ole. "He yust got out of da hospital."

Little Ole was talking to his grandpa one day.

"Grampa Olson, vat position do you play on da football team?"

"I'm too old to play football, Little Ole," his grandpa replied.

"Dat's funny," said Little Ole. "Papa said ve could afford to go on vacation as soon as you kicked off."

Ole: In da army, my drill sergeant said I'd never amount to
anyting. He should see me now: I've amounted to
nearly two hundred pounds.

OLE AND THE ARMY

As Ole was leaving Basic Training, he said goodbye to his drill sergeant.

The sergeant challenged Ole by replying, "Olson, I know you never liked me. I'll bet you can hardly wait for the day I die, so you can come back and SPIT on my grave."

Ole replied, "Oh, no, Drill Sergeant. I vould never do dat. I promised myself vonce I got out of da army, I'd never stand in a long line again."

Ole: I had a girlfriend vile I vas in da army. I wrote her every day for six months, only she told me she vas goin' to marry somevon else. I wrote back to see who she vas marryin'. It vas da mailman.

Ole: In da army, I vas brought up for an offense. Dey gave me da choice of von month's restriction or twenty days' pay. I said, "Okay, I'll take da money."

Ole was on guard duty one day, when a general was chauffeured to the gate. He wanted to pass through Ole's station. Ole insisted that the general tell him the password or Ole couldn't let him through.

Finally, the general got impatient and told his driver to drive on. Ole came in close to the general and whispered, "I'm kinda new at dis, General. Do I shoot you or da driver?"

Little Lena: My piano teacher is very religious.

Lena: Oh, vy do you tink dat?

Little Lena: Every time I play, she closes her eyes and says, "Oh, Lordy!"

OLE & LENA'S CHILDREN

Ingeborg: Oh, Lena, dat new baby is da spittin' image of his fadder.

Lena: Vat do you care, so long as he's healthy?

Lena: Vat did you learn in Sunday School today, Little Ole?

Little Ole: Vell, ve learned how Moses vent behind enemy lines to rescue da Jewish people from da Egyptians. First, Moses ordered dem engineers to build a pontoon bridge. Den, after da people crossed, he sent bombers back to blow up da bridge, and da Egyptian tanks ver followin' dem.

Lena: Little Ole, did your teacher really tell you dat?

Little Ole: Vell, no, Mama, but if I told you vat she really said about Moses and da Red Sea, you'd never belief it.

Little Ole: I failed every subject except algebra.

Lena: How did you stop from failin' algebra?

Little Ole: I didn't take algebra.

Ole: Dis service has gone on so long dat my butt's fallen asleep.

Lena: Yah, I know, Ole. I heard it snore three times.

OLE & LENA AND CHURCH

Lena: Ole likes to go to church because dey usually sing his favorite hymn: "Ole, Ole, Ole."

Ole attended church one Sunday. The pastor greeted him after the service with a question: "Won't you join the Army of the Lord?"

Ole replied, "I'm already in da Army of da Lord."

"How come I don't see you except on Christmas and Easter?" asked the pastor.

Ole whispered back, "I'm in da secret service."

Satan appeared at First Lutheran Church where Ole was sitting in the front pew. Everyone hung back in fear, except for Ole, who approached the Devil.

"Aren't you afraid of me?" Satan asked.

"Heck, no," said Ole, "I've been married to your sister for twenty-five years."

Ole and Sven were at church, and the pastor said, "Everybody who wants to go to heaven stand up."

Everyone but Ole and Sven stood. When the pastor asked why Ole didn't want to go to heaven, Ole said, "I do. I yust tought you ver takin' a load up dere now, and ve're not ready yet."

Lena: I've had it, Ole—*NO MORE YOKES ABOUT MY WEIGHT!*

Ole: Okay, Lena, but who else could burn out five refrigerator bulbs in von month?

OLE & LENA'S LEFTOVERS

Lena: Ole vas named "Norvegian Man of da Year." Dat shows you vat kind of year it's been.

Sven and Ole were out hunting, and another hunter spotted them dragging a deer toward their truck.

"Hey guys," the hunter called to them, "if you drag that deer in the other direction, the antlers won't dig into the ground."

After the hunter left, Sven and Ole decided to try it.

"Dat guy vas right. Dis is a lot easier," said Ole.

"Yah," Sven replied, "but ve're gettin' fardder away from da truck."

Ole: I am a man of few vords.

Sven: Yah, I'm married, too.

Ole: I vish I could get in von more dig at Ingeborg before dis book is over.

Lena: Vy? She's been dietin', and I tink she looks good.

Ole: Lena, da only ting dat could make Ingeborg look good is distance.

THE GREAT DEBATE

Ole: Lena, I am from a smaller town dan you are.

Lena: Oh, no you're not, Ole! My town is smaller.

Ole: Oh, yeah? In my town, dey didn't use yellow pages. Dey yust used von yellow Post-It.

Lena: My town's power plant vas a Diehard Battery.

Ole: In my town, da all-night diner vas open 'til 2:30 p.m.

Lena: My town is so small dat da road map says, "Actual size."

Ole: Mine is so small dat it's only open three days a veek.

Lena: Ve had only von streetlight and da last von to bed had to turn it off.

Ole: Our sanitation department vas a giant Q-Tip.

Lena: My town's heavy industry vas a three-hundred-pound Avon Lady.

Ole: My town vas so small dat ve had to share a town drunk vit da next town.

Lena: Ole, I guarantee you dat *MY* town is smaller!

Ole: And I'm sure dat *MY* town is smaller!

Lena: You vanna bet?

Ole: Lena, I yust tought of someting: You and me are from da same town.

Lena: Oh, dat's right. Small vorld, isn't it?

Are You Norvegian?

(Take Ole & Lena's quiz to find out.
Ve hope you do better dan dey did.)

1. MAZE CHALLENGE

Ole loves vatchin' da television. Can you help him find da remote control?

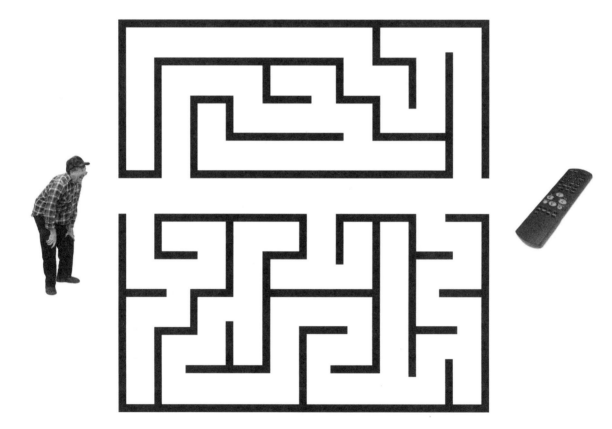

If dis puzzle takes you more dan five minutes, you may be Norvegian.

2. WHICH IS NOT LIKE THE OTHERS?

Can you find da von picture dat is different dan da udders?

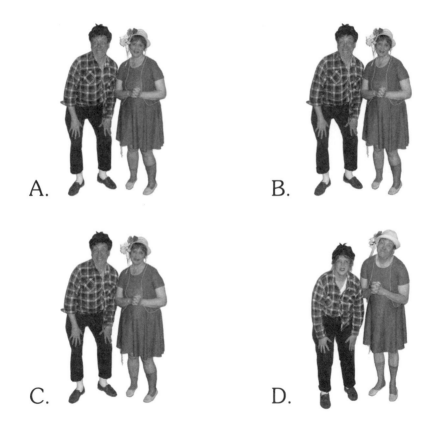

A. B.

C. D.

If dey all look da same to you, den you're probably Norvegian.

3. WORD SCRAMBLE

Fix da vords on da left, and match dem vit da vords on da right. Da first von is done for you.

I————————————I

em	me
leO	Ole
enaL	Lena
venS	Sven
ngeborgI	Ingeborg
ttleLi leO	Little Ole
ttleLi enaL	Little Lena
orvegianN	Norwegian

If you get more dan von right, you are vay too smart to be Norwegian.

4. CROSSWORD PUZZLE

Can you finish dis crossvord puzzle usin' da given clues?

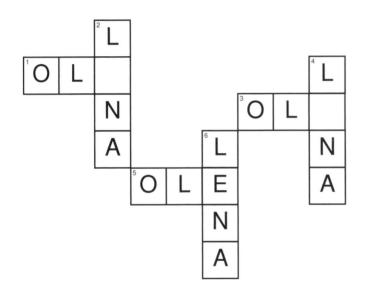

ACROSS

1. Lena's "stud"

3. He's not as sharp as a nail

5. It takes a lot of hard work to be as lazy as he is

DOWN

2. Ole's "hot dish"

4. She's really cookin' (at least she tries)

6. Her leftovers make perfect building materials

If you can't figure dis von out, join da club!

5. CRYPTOGRAM

Dis von's called a cryptogram. Dat means it's written in code. Can you solve da cryptogram below?

HINT: *Da letter A has been done for you.*

<u>A</u> <u>_</u> <u>_</u> <u>_</u> <u>_</u> <u>A</u> <u>_</u> <u>_</u> <u>_</u> <u>_</u> <u>_</u>
L A R S   I S   S O   D U M B   T H A T   H E   T H I N K S

<u>_</u> <u>A</u> <u>_</u> <u>_</u> <u>A</u> <u>_</u> <u>_</u> <u>A</u> <u>_</u> <u>_</u> <u>A</u> <u>'</u> <u>_</u> <u>_</u> <u>_</u>!
J O A N   O F   A R C   W A S   N O A H S   W I F E

A = A	G = G	M = M	S = S	Y = Y
B = B	H = H	N = N	T = T	Z = Z
C = C	I = I	O = O	U = U	
D = D	J = J	P = P	V = V	
E = E	K = K	Q = Q	W = W	
F = F	L = L	R = R	X = X	

Are you as confused as ve are? UFFDA!

6. COLOR BY NUMBER

Use da key below to color dis picture, and reveal a place dat's very special to da Olson family.

1 =	Green
2 =	Blue
3 =	Brown
4 =	Tan

If dis looks like da scene in your back yard, yup, ve're related.

Bruce's Biography:

Bruce and his wife, Judy, have been married for more than thirty-five years. The couple resides in Cambridge, Minnesota, where they both work for the Cambridge-Isanti School District. Bruce teaches math and speech communications, as well as directing the high school musical, serving as an advisor for the Battle of the Bands and the student variety show, and co-hosting the annual faculty variety show. Bruce is a retired Sergeant Major of the National Guard, with more than thirty-three years of service. He enjoys making stained glass and spending time with his wife and two miniature schnauzers, Harry and Sam. At left is a photo from Bruce's son and daughter-in-law's wedding in August of 2005. Matthew played Little Ole for ten years. Both Matthew and his wife, Jennifer, are teachers.

Ann's Biography:

Ann lives in the small Minnesota town of Cambridge with Larry, her husband of thirty-one years. In addition to teaching science at the local middle school, Ann works as an educational consultant and makes various appearances in her role as Lena. Ann enjoys spending her free time with her three grown sons at the family cabin "up north."